Step-by-Step
Mosaics

Michelle Powell

Heinemann Library
Chicago, Illinois

Published by Heinemann Library,
an imprint of Reed Educational & Professional Publishing,
Chicago, IL
Customer Service 888-454-2279
Visit our website at www.heinemannlibrary.com

Photographs and design copyright © Search Press Limited 2001
Text copyright © Michelle Powell 2001
Originated by Graphics '91, Singapore
Designed by Search Press
Printed in China

07 06 05 04
10 9 8 7 6 5 4 3 2

Library of Congress Cataloging-in-Publication Data
Powell, Michelle, 1971-
   Mosaics / Michelle Powell.
     p. cm. -- (Step-by-step)
   Includes bibliographical references and index.
   ISBN 1-57572-332-8 (library binding)
   ISBN 1-4034-0710-X (paperback binding)
   1. Mosaics--Technique--Juvenile literature. [1. Mosaics--Technique. 2. Handicraft.] I.
Title. II. Step-by-step (Heinemann Library)
   TT910 .P69 2001
   738.5--dc21

00-046192

Acknowledgments
The author and publishers are grateful to the following for permission to reproduce copyright material:
Bridgeman Art Library, p.5.

Photographs: Search Press Studios

This book is dedicated to all my family, but mostly to Gemma, Hayley, Rikki, Tara, Dan, Lynsey, James and Natalie.

Some words are shown in bold, **like this**. You can find out what they mean by looking in the glossary.

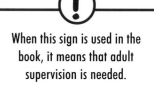

When this sign is used in the book, it means that adult supervision is needed.

REMEMBER!
Ask an adult to help you when you see this sign.

Contents

3

Introduction

Traditional mosaics are beautiful works of art. They are created with many small pieces of clay, glass, stone, and other hard materials that are set closely together on a firm surface to create a **decorative** design or picture.

The earliest mosaics date back to 3000 B.C., when they were usually created as a type of floor decoration made of small colored pebbles. Later, glass, marble, and clay were colored and cut into small cubes or tiles. These tiles were used to decorate the floors, walls, and ceilings of important buildings. A thick layer of plaster would be applied to the wall, and then a picture or design was painted on the surface while the plaster was still wet. Before the plaster dried, matching colored cubes or tiles were pushed into the surface to create the mosaic.

Large mosaics took a long time to make and were expensive, so they were very precious and a sign of great wealth. They were mostly used to decorate the inside of churches and religious buildings. Early Christian mosaics show figures and animals with decorative borders. In Islam, temples were decorated with beautiful designs of leaves and palm trees with a vibrant gold background. The Greeks often decorated their floors with dark and light pebble mosaics.

The ancient Egyptians made mosaic jewelry for their kings by setting tiny pieces of **turquoise**, precious stones, and **enamel** into gold. On page 16 you will see how you can create a similar piece of jewelry using pasta painted gold and turquoise. Gold and turquoise were also used to decorate statues and pottery items made by the ancient craft workers of Latin America. The Greeks and Romans made huge mosaics from handmade colored clay tiles. The coaster project on page 20 shows you how to make your own clay mosaic tiles.

Some early mosaics can still be seen today, as they have not worn away over time. Now, special small colored glass squares and highly glazed clay tiles are made, and although mosaics take a long time to create and are very expensive, they are still being made by skilled crafts people.

Opposite *The best-known mosaics were made by Roman and Byzantine craft workers. The mosaic pictured on the right was designed to decorate the church of Saint Vitale in Ravenna, Italy, in about A.D. 530. It shows soldiers at the court of the Byzantine Emperor Justinian. Large mosaics were probably designed by companies of artists, and the pieces, the tessarae, were cut before being taken to a building to be stuck in place.*

4

Materials

The items pictured here are the basic tools and equipment you will need to make the projects shown in this book. Mosaics can be created using many different small objects. You will already have some of these materials at home. Other items will be easy to find in your local stores. In addition, specific items are needed for certain projects, such as elastic cord, a felt tip pen, a wooden rolling pin, cord, pliers, sequins, colored metallic trim, and feathers. Check the list of materials carefully before you start each project.

Note Whenever you use paints, glue, or clay, you should cover your work area with newspaper. Wear old clothes and work on a clean, flat surface. Have a damp cloth ready in case you spill, and be sure to clean up when you have finished creating your mosaic.

All sorts of things can be decorated with mosaics. *Wood,* **terracotta,** and *cardboard* are ideal, but so are *fabric, paper,* and *cookies.*

It is possible to create mosaics with all sorts of materials. You can use *pebbles,* **high-density foam,** *cardboard, posterboard* and *felt,* and even *eggshells, pasta,* and *candy.* Wonderful mosaic effects can be created with other things too—*air-drying clay, foil,* and even *chains, screws, washers, nuts,* and *bolts.*

Mosaic designs can be secured using *multipurpose glue*, a *glue stick*, or *fabric glue*—be sure to read the manufacturer's instructions carefully. Use *icing* when sticking candy to cookies. Icing is made by mixing powdered sugar and lemon juice in a *bowl*.

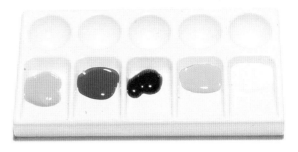

A **palette** is useful for paints, but an old plate will do just as well. *Water-based paint* is used for the projects in this book. *Colored pens* can be used instead of paint if you wish.

A *coffee stirrer* is used to measure and adjust the gaps between mosaic pieces.

Scissors are used to cut paper, card, foil, fabric, cordboard, and string.

A *hole punch* is used to make neat, round holes.

Large and small *paintbrushes* are used to apply glue and paint.

A *knife* is used for cutting clay and *spoons* for mixing *lemon juice* and *powdered sugar*.

A *ruler* is used as a guide when drawing straight lines and when trimming clay.

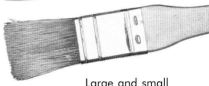

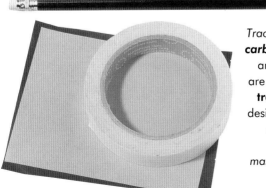

Tracing paper, **carbon paper,** and a *pencil* are used when **transferring** designs. These are held in place with *masking tape*.

Newspaper is used to cover your work surface.

Insect Greeting Card

It is very easy to make attractive mosaic greeting cards for your family and friends using your own drawings or paintings. Make sure you paint or draw them on thick cardboard using brightly colored, bold designs. Strong images and patterns work best, as fine detail will be lost when the picture is cut into mosaic pieces. Draw a grid on the front of the picture or photograph, as in step 4, and cut along the lines to create your mosaic pieces.

YOU WILL NEED

Thin cardboard
Medium weight cardboard
Carbon paper • Tracing paper
Masking tape • Pencil
Scissors • Ruler
Water-based paints or colored pens
Paintbrush • Glue stick
Coffee stirrer

1 Fold a piece of thin cardboard in half and place it to one side.

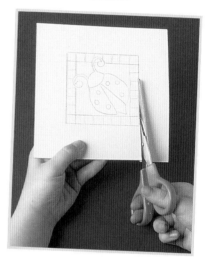

2 **Transfer** the insect pattern shown on page 29 to a piece of medium weight cardboard. Cut around the edge.

3 Use colored paints or pens to fill in the design.

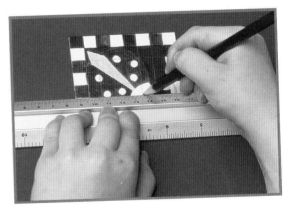

4 Use a pencil and ruler to join up the lines on the border—to form a grid on the front of the design.

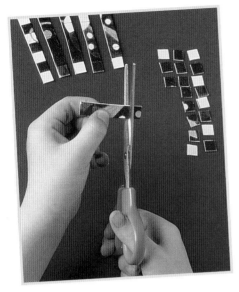

5

Cut along each line using scissors. Carefully lay the pieces down in order as you cut them out.

6

Carefully glue the pieces in the right order to the front of the folded card. Leave a small gap between each piece, using a coffee stirrer as a guide.

FURTHER IDEAS

Use a color photocopy of a favorite photograph instead of drawing your own picture.

African Mask

Masks were often worn in African tribal dances. The dancers would also use body **adornments** and sometimes special clothing, which added to the drama and atmosphere of the dance. You can make your own African mosaic mask using small squares and triangles of thin, colored **high-density foam**, felt, or thin cardboard. These soft materials are excellent for masks because they are more comfortable than some of the harder materials that are available.

YOU WILL NEED

Colored high-density foam
Carbon paper • Tracing paper
Masking tape • Pencil
Scissors • Felt tipped pen
Multipurpose glue • Hole punch
Elastic cord

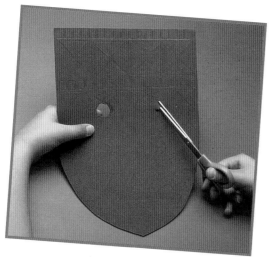

Transfer the mask pattern shown on page 29 to a piece of high-density foam. Cut around the basic shape. Hold the mask up to your face, and carefully feel around on the front for the position of your eyes. Ask a friend to mark their position with a felt-tipped pen. Then cut out the eye holes using scissors.

2 Use the pattern as a rough guide. Choosing different colors, cut squares, triangles, and wedge shapes from high-density foam.

3 Glue the pieces to the mask using multipurpose glue.

Cut out a nose from another piece of high-density foam and glue it into position. Cut out two circles for the nostrils and glue them to the nose. Let the glue dry for half an hour.

5 Use a hole punch to make a hole on either side of the mask, approximately ½ inch (1cm) from the edge.

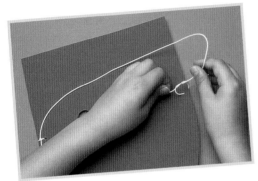

6 Cut a piece of elastic cord long enough to fit around your head. Tie each end through the holes in the mask.

FURTHER IDEAS

Choose an animal and make a fun mask, or choose different colors and create your own African mask.

Knight in Armor Picture

In the Middle Ages battling knights wore armor made of metal sheets and **chain mail**, which protected them from injury. In order to make this knight look more realistic, metal nuts, bolts, screws, washers, and chain are used, along with colored and silver foil. You do not have to use all of these—just create the knight with whatever you have. Real chain has been used to create the chain mail. You can buy this from most craft and home improvement stores.

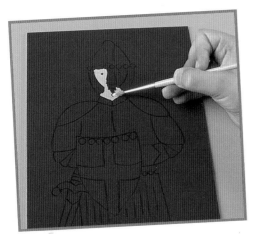

Transfer the knight in armor and shield patterns shown on page 29 to a piece of cardboard. Paint the knight's face using a small paintbrush.

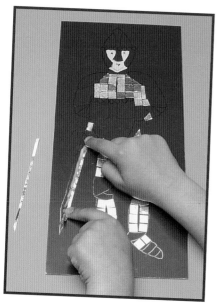

Glue the foil to the knight using multipurpose glue.

Cut silver foil into small squares, triangles, and wedge shapes for the armor. Cut out two strips long enough for the sword.

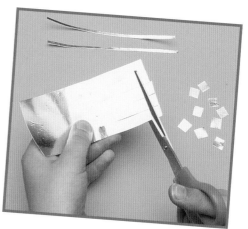

Roll pieces of silver foil into small balls. Glue them to the cuff on the armor and to the helmet.

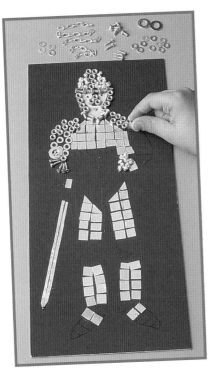

Position the nuts, bolts, washers, screws, and chain carefully on the knight. Glue in place.

> **!**
>
> If you decide to include chain, ask an adult to pull it apart with pliers, to make the correct lengths.

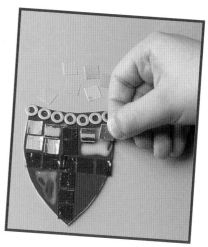

6 Cut out squares of colored foil. Decorate the shield with the squares and washers. Then glue them into position with multipurpose glue. Allow the glue to dry overnight.

FURTHER IDEAS

Make a metal robot picture using the same techniques, or create a shiny alien.

13

Indian Elephant Shoebag

In India, elephants wearing bright, colorful decorative **saddlecloths** and elaborate headdresses are often seen at festivals. Using colored felt or fabric, feathers, and pretty gold or metallic colored trim, you can create a fabric Indian elephant mosaic on a plain shoe or toiletries bag. If you do not have one that is suitable, ask an adult to make a simple bag out of a rectangle of fabric. Fold this in half, sew the bottom edges together, and then sew the side edges. Turn the top edge over to the inside to form a hem, and sew along the bottom edge, leaving a gap at the side seam. Thread cord through the hem and tie a knot at the end.

YOU WILL NEED
Fabric shoebag
Gray and colored felt
Carbon paper • Tracing paper
Masking tape • Pencil
Two small feathers • Sequins
Metallic colored trim
Scissors • Multipurpose glue

 1 Cut gray felt into small squares and wedge shapes.

2 **Transfer** the elephant design shown on page 30 to your shoebag. Attach the gray felt squares and wedge shapes to the elephant using multipurpose glue.

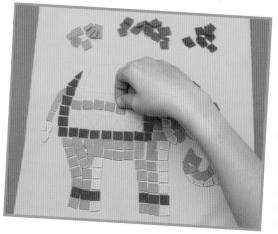

3 Use different colors and cut some more felt into small squares and wedge shapes. Glue them in position.

Use multipurpose glue to attach small feathers to the headdress, and use sequins to decorate the saddlecloth.

5 Glue metallic colored trim around the headdress and the base of the saddlecloth.

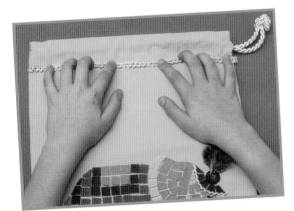

6 Glue metallic colored trim around the top of the bag to decorate it. Allow the glue to dry overnight.

Note The design on this shoebag is only glued on, and therefore, the bag should not be washed. If it gets dirty, carefully sponge it clean.

FURTHER IDEAS

Decorate a pencil case, school bag, baseball hat, T-shirt, or jacket. Change the colors for different effects.

Egyptian Eagle Necklace

Beautiful gold and precious stone jewelry has been found in the tombs of ancient Egyptian **pharaohs.** You can make your own dazzling Egyptian mosaic jewelry using dried pasta—all sorts of different shapes are available. Look for small shells and tubes that can be threaded like beads on elastic cord. The pasta is painted using colored and metallic water-based paints in the same colors as the gold and precious stones used in Egyptian jewelry.

Transfer the eagle pattern shown on page 30 to cardboard. Carefully cut it out.

Cover your work surface with newspaper. Paint the pasta shells and tubes with metallic and colored paint. Let the paint dry and wash your hands thoroughly.

Note Do not cook or eat the pasta after it has been painted.

Use a hole punch to make three holes at the edge of both the eagle's wings.

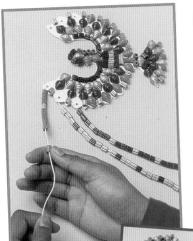

5

Tie three lengths of elastic cord through the holes on one side of one wing. Thread pasta tubes onto the elastic.

Note String can be used instead of elastic.

4 Glue the pasta shells and tubes in place using multipurpose glue.

6 Thread the other end of each piece of elastic cord through the remaining three holes and tie securely. Glue on more shells to cover the holes.

FURTHER IDEAS

Create a **scarab beetle** bracelet to match your necklace using the same techniques. Or look for other Egyptian designs and make your own jewelry using different colors.

Math Cookies

Mosaics can even be created using **edible** items like the small colored candy in this project. Here, candy-coated chocolate is attached to plain cookies using icing. The quantities given make enough icing for four large cookies. If you want to decorate more, you will need to make more icing. Use everyday spoons to make the icing, and remember to wash your hands well before you start.

YOU WILL NEED

Large plain cookies
Small colored candy
Powdered sugar
Lemon juice
Bowl • Spoon

 Place six heaping spoonfuls of powdered sugar into a bowl.

 Add four spoonfuls of lemon juice.

 Stir the sugar and lemon juice together until all the lumps are gone.

Note The icing should be like a stiff paste. If it is too runny, add more powdered sugar. If it is too dry, add a drop more lemon juice.

4 Spoon a small quantity of icing over a cookie and use the back of a spoon to spread it out.

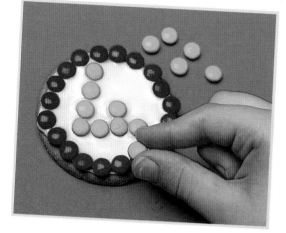

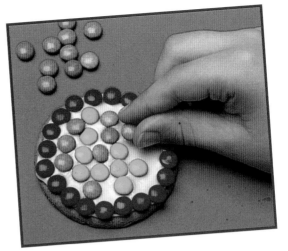

5 Press colored candy into the wet icing around the edge of the cookie. Use a different color to create a number in the middle.

6 Fill in the spaces around the number with a third color. Leave the cookies until the icing is set.

FURTHER IDEAS
Why not mosaic your name on top of your birthday cake, or decorate some cookies with simple shapes.

Grecian Coaster

The Greeks and Romans used small clay tiles to make their mosaics. In this project mosaic tiles are made using air-drying clay. The rolled out clay is soft enough to cut with a knife. Most of the pieces are either squares or triangles, so the design can only have straight edges. When the clay is dry, it is painted with traditional Greek colors and the coaster is then sealed with multipurpose glue to protect it.

YOU WILL NEED

Air-drying clay • Cardboard
Newspaper • Knife
Wooden rolling pin • Ruler
Water-based paint
Large and small paintbrushes
Scissors • Multipurpose glue

1 Cover your work surface with newspaper. Take a ball of clay, roughly the size of a tennis ball, and roll it out to a thickness of about ¼ inch (0.5cm).

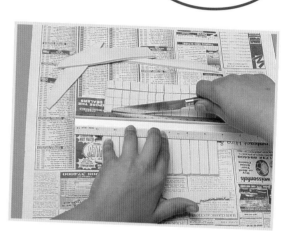

2 Trim off the edges of the clay with a knife, using a ruler as a guide. Cut vertical lines approximately ½ inch (1cm) apart. Cut horizontal lines in the same way to form small clay squares.

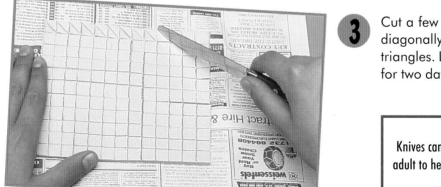

3 Cut a few of the squares diagonally to make triangles. Let the clay dry for two days.

Knives can be sharp. Ask an adult to help you cut the clay.

Use a small paintbrush and different colors to paint the squares and triangles.

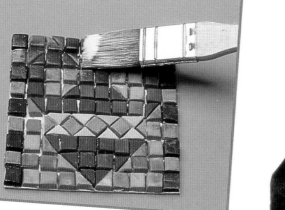

5 Cut out a piece of cardboard roughly 4¼ inches (11cm) square. Using the design shown on page 30 as a guide, start to build the mosaic design. Secure the tiles with multipurpose glue and work line by line.

6 Continue adding lines of tiles to complete the design. Apply a coat of PVA glue all over the tiles using a large paintbrush. Leave to dry overnight.

Note When glue is dry, it can be very difficult to remove, so wear an apron or old shirt to protect your clothes.

FURTHER IDEAS

You can make matching place mats and hot pads using this technique.

Seaside Pebble Frame

Small pebbles are great for making mosaics. You can sometimes find colored ones on the beach, but you could paint the pebbles yourself if you can not find any. Here, white pebbles about the size of a pea and very small pebbles that have been painted after they have been glued down have been used. **Pearlescent** paint can be used for a shimmering effect, which makes the picture frame look more colorful. Choose a frame with a very wide and flat border to give you plenty of space for your design, and use it to display your own drawing, painting, or photograph.

YOU WILL NEED

Plain wooden frame
Selection of small pebbles
Newspaper • **Carbon paper**
Tracing paper • Masking tape
Pencil • Water-based paint
Paintbrush
Multipurpose glue

1 **Transfer** the patterns shown on page 31 to your frame. Draw some waves in the background and then paint them, working from the top to the bottom.

2 Apply multipurpose glue around the edge of the starfish, over the fish's body, and around the edge of the fish's tail.

3 Sprinkle very small pebbles over the wet glue to decorate the starfish and fish. Let the glue dry for at least fifteen minutes.

 Tip the frame over a piece of newspaper to remove excess pebbles. These can be saved and used for another project.

5 Paint the small pebbles on the fish and the starfish in colors of your choice.

6 Apply glue to the center of the starfish. Add stripes of glue to the fish's body and tail, and lines of glue following the shape of the waves. Press larger pebbles into the glue, and let the glue dry overnight.

FURTHER IDEAS
Cover the top of a box, or make other decorative pebble pictures using this technique.

Celestial Pot

All sorts of materials can be used to create a mosaic. Here broken eggshells are glued to a plain **terracotta** plant pot. The theme is the sky—one side shows a sun, the other a moon and star. For a small pot like this you will need the shells of three eggs. If your pot is larger, you will need more. Use the completed pot for an indoor plant, as the mosaic will not be weatherproof.

1 Wash the eggshells in warm water and place them on newspaper to dry.

2 Break the eggshells carefully into large pieces, then paint them with different colors. Let the paint dry.

3 **Transfer** the patterns shown on page 31 to your pot. Apply multipurpose glue to one area of the design.

4 Break the eggshells into smaller pieces. Firmly press one of the pieces into the wet glue to break the shell further.

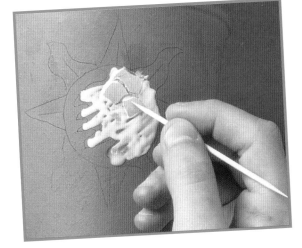

5 Use a coffee stirrer to push the pieces of eggshell apart, leaving small gaps between them.

6 Continue applying different colors to your design. Finish by filling in around the design with more eggshells and allow the glue to dry.

FURTHER IDEAS
Create a beautiful jewelry box by decorating a plain wooden box with brightly colored eggshells.

Aztec Book Cover

This book cover is inspired by the wonderful colors of the Aztecs. You can transform a plain, bound notebook easily with this bold geometric pattern. Detailed mosaic designs can take many hours to complete, but here the design is very quick; the mosaic is created on a printing block that is then used to print the pattern over and over again. You can use many colors on this block and print instant designs.

YOU WILL NEED
Plain book
High-density foam
Cardboard • Scissors
Water-based paint
Paintbrush • Cord • Bead
Multipurpose glue

 1

Cut high-density foam into small squares and triangles, using the design on page 31 as a rough guide.

2 Cut out a square of cardboard roughly the size of the design. Glue the foam pieces to the cardboard using multipurpose glue, following the lines of the design, to create a printing block. Let the glue dry.

3 Apply a thin layer of paint to the foam squares and triangles using a small paintbrush and colors of your choice.

4

Press the printing block to the front of your book.

5 Repeat step 4, applying more paint each time. Complete a stripe down one side of the book. Let the paint dry.

6 Loop a length of cord around the book, and thread both ends through a tightly fitting bead to secure it.

FURTHER IDEAS

Create your own mosaic design using different shapes, and stamp the design on a picture frame.

Patterns

You can trace the patterns on these pages straight from the book (step 1). You can also make them larger or smaller on a photocopier if you wish, and then follow steps 2–4.

! Ask an adult to help you enlarge the patterns on a photocopier.

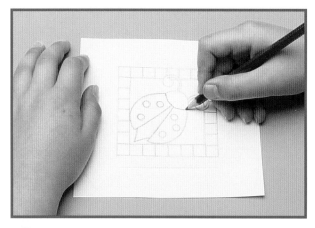

1 Place a piece of tracing paper over the pattern and tape it down with small pieces of masking tape. Trace around the outline using a soft pencil.

2 Place **carbon paper** face down on the surface you want to transfer the design to. Place the tracing or photocopy over the top and tape it in place.

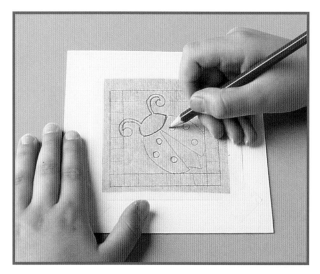

3 Trace over the outline with a pencil.

4 Remove the tracing paper and carbon paper to reveal the transferred image.

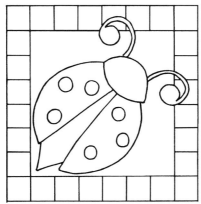

These patterns are for the Insect Greeting Cards featured on pages 8–9.

These patterns are for the Knight in Armor Picture featured on pages 12–13.

This pattern is for the African Mask featured on pages 10–11.

This pattern is for the Indian Elephant Shoebag featured on pages 14–15.

This pattern is for the Egyptian Eagle Necklace featured on pages 16–17.

This pattern is for the Grecian Coaster featured on pages 20–21.

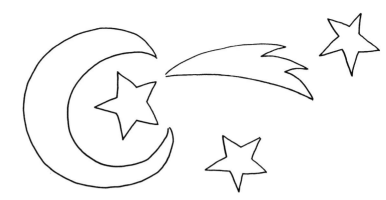

These patterns are for the Celestial Pot featured on pages 24–25.

This pattern is for the Aztec Book Cover featured on pages 26–27.

These patterns are for the Seaside Pebble Frame featured on pages 22–23.

Glossary

Adornment   something that adds to the attractiveness of someone or something

Carbon paper   paper with a dark coating that is placed between two pieces of plain paper so that pencil marks on the top piece of paper go through to the second piece

Chain mail   type of armor made from closely linked metal chain

Decorative   something made purely for the way it looks

Edible   able to be eaten

Enamel   shiny, colorful paint applied to metal or pottery by heating it

High-density foam   special kind of foam used in arts and crafts that is sold at craft stores

Palette   thin wooden board or plastic dish used to hold and mix different colors of paint

Pearlescent   having a soft shine like a pearl

Pharoah   ancient Egyptian king

Saddlecloth   cloth placed over a horse or other animal

Scarab beetle   type of brightly colored beetle; Egyptian carving or jewelry in the shape of a beetle

Terracotta   "cooked earth"; orange-colored clay formed into pots or other containers and baked until hard and dry

Transfer   to move something from one place to another

Turquoise   greenish-blue stone used by many cultures in making jewelry

More Books to Read

Avi-Yonah, Michael and Avi Avi-Yonah. *Piece by Piece!: Mosaics of the Ancient World.* Minneapolis, Minn.: Lerner, 1993.

Emberley, Ed. *Mosaic: A Step by Step Cut & Paste Drawing Book.* New York: Little, Brown & Co., 1995.

Kelly, Sarah. *Amazing Mosaics.* Hauppauge, N.Y.: Barron's Educational Series, Inc., 2000.

Index